D1569379

First published in 2004 by immprint
Artwork © Wayne Lloyd/immprint

The contributors to this publication and its contents
assert their moral right to be identified as authors in
accordance with sections 77 and 78 of the UK Copyright,
Designs and Patents Act 1988.

ISBN 1-903781-07-8

British Library Cataloguing in Publication Data.
A catalogue record for this book is available from the
British Library.

Illustrations by Wayne Winner
Designed by Keith Sargent

Printed in Singapore 2004.

Published by immprint (2004)
immprint
+44[0]20 7702 7613
www.immprint.com

Wayne Winner's
Arthouse
CINEMA
#1

an immprint publication

Social Services

The

Medication

Day Trip

Rules

Wheelchair Ramp

Self Destruct

Idiots

Sing Cuckoo
Sing Cuckoo

Residence of Lord Summerisle

The Church

Phallic Hedge

Summerisle Hote

The

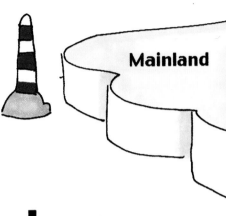

Mainland

Wicker

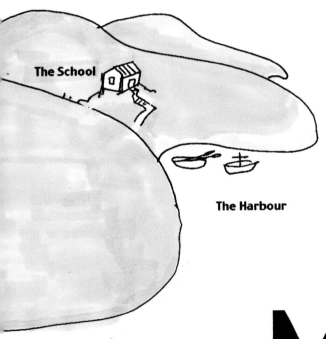

The School

The Harbour

Man

On a mission to Summerisle

on the island

Never seen her before, honest....

My name is Sergeant Howie and I'm looking for this girl. We received an anonymous tip off that she's dead.

Later...

God Save Us!

CROAK!

Grandma, what's a phallus?

A massive erect penis, dear

gasp!

At the pub...

Can I have a room for the...

She's my daughter- isn't she lovely?

Show us your knickers tra la la

What are these?

Our Harvest Time 'Virgins'

This one got broken...

That night

Knock tap tap Knock

what the...

Knock

9

Knock

And Out of the Window...

Lord Have Mercy!

Next Morning

Lord Sommerisle, I've come to complain about the filthy members in your society. And to find this girl.

Oh I remember now. She's buried in the churchyard.

At the unconsecrated ground...

There is just a dead hare in her coffin, where is she?

Well, I'm off to dance in the May Day Celebrations. See Ya!

May Day Celebrations? Sweet Lord On High! She is a human SACRIFICE!!!

Later... WHACK!

This costume will do for me!

I'll follow his lordship and set her free

heh heh

ss

There she is!

Hiya

DA NA!

You are all nicked!

HA HA HA HA HA HA HA

Five Minutes Later...

Sing Cuckoo ♫ Sing Cuckoo ♫

DOH!

13

West

TEUTONIA

Alexander

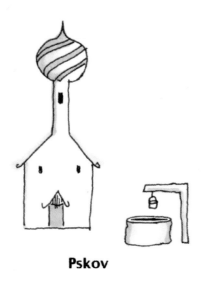

Pskov

South

North

Frozen Lake

Nevsky

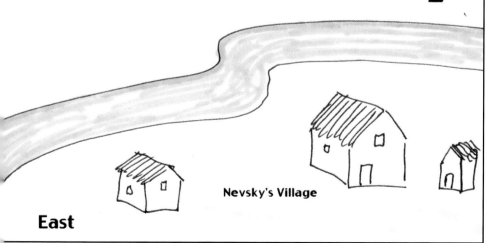

Nevsky's Village

East

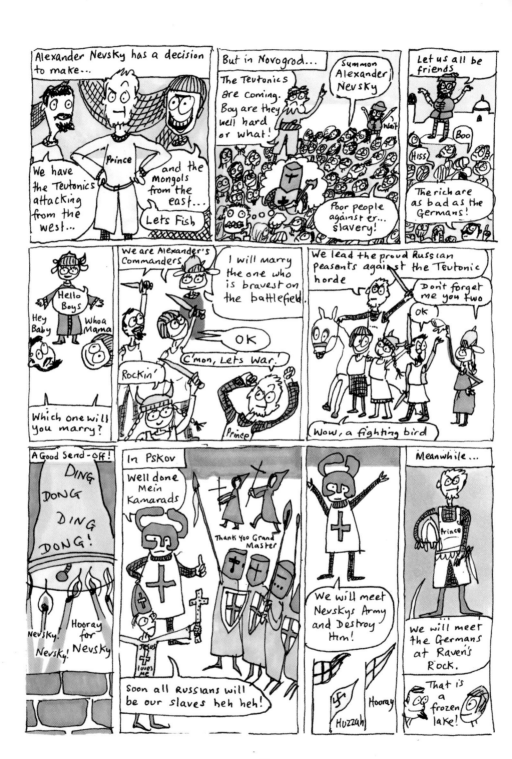

Tower Hill

Seat of Sir Robert Dudley in Lov

The Church of England

Elizabeth's Palace

Elizabeth

Walsingham's Castle

Whatever

The Spotlight

Fame

History

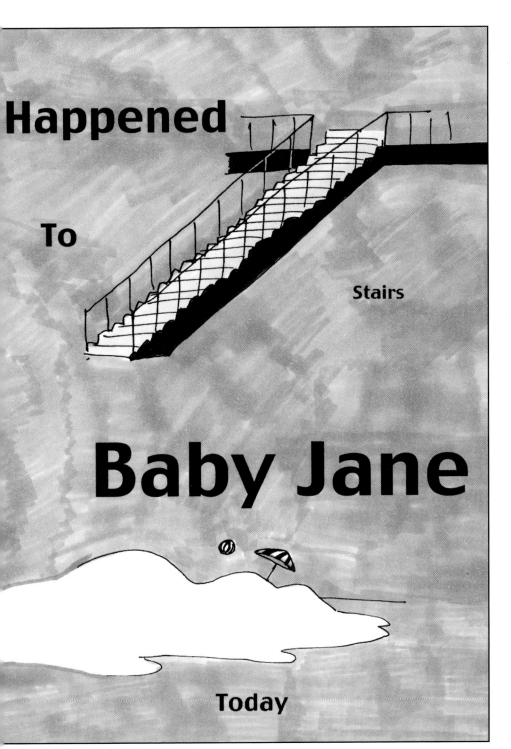

Happened

To

Stairs

Baby Jane

Today

The Phone Box

Red Paint

Disguise

What a Night

The Country

Turner's Head

Earls Court, in a Dream

Performance

Replicant Laboratory

Blade

The Derelict

Street Market

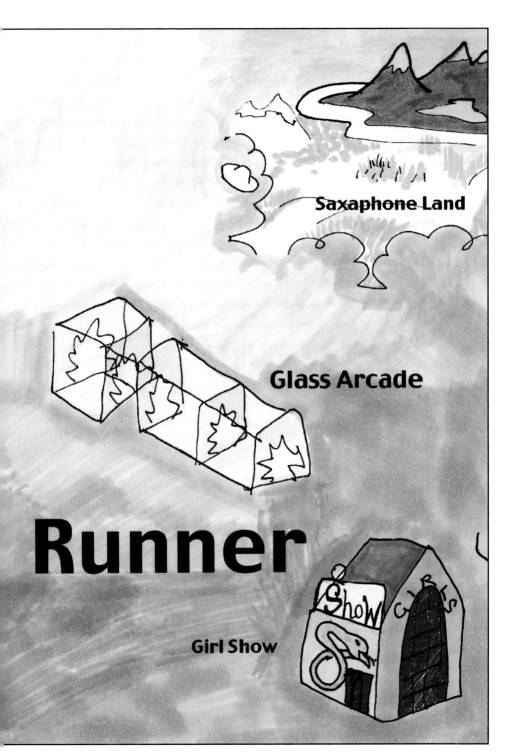

Saxaphone Land

Glass Arcade

Runner

Girl Show

SHOW GIRLS

Take me to your friend Tyrell...

OK

At Tyrell's...

Give me more life, fucker...

You have shone so very very brightly Roy...

DIE DAD

OW!

and you..

erg!

Back at Sebastien's apartment...

Nooooo!

Uh oh

BLAM

2 minutes later

Reckon life is pretty important huh?

Soon all my memories will be lost, like tears in the rain... time to die

Flutter....

Phew!

Back at Deckard's

Let's split Rachel. I think I might be a replicant...

I knew it

Overland Hotel

The

Room 374

Bar

Rocky Mountains

Here's Johnny

Shining

Maze

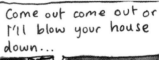

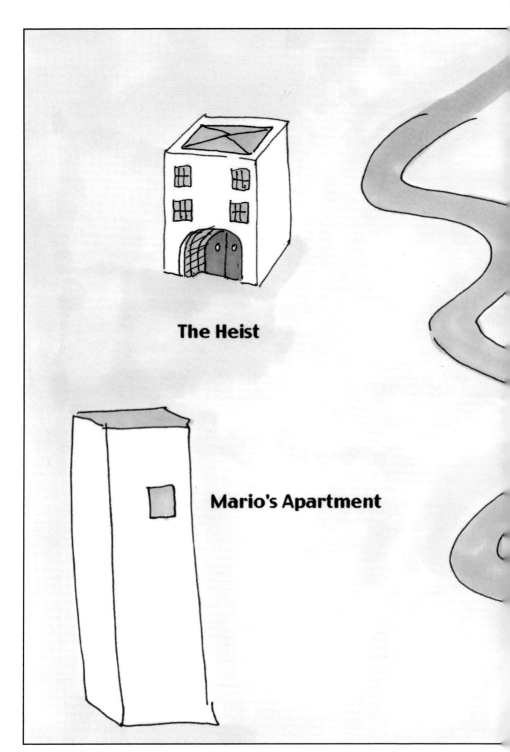

The Heist

Mario's Apartment

Rough And Tumble

Rififi

The Long Road Home

45

The

Outer Space

Mountain Laboratory

Demon

The Harris House

Seed

You are to be the mother of my child.

Doctor Harris and I had a child, but she died of Leukaemia!

5 Minutes later...

Oh no!

snip snip

CLUNK

2 minutes later

HOW WAS IT FOR YOU?

crap

IN 28 DAYS YOU WILL GIVE BIRTH

Got any ice cream with anchovies?

28 days later...

No

Can I see it?

At the lab...

Proteus is taking knowledge from the universe.

... and he's got a terminal at your house to play with...

Oops!

At the house

Proteus and I have had a baby!

In the basement

Proteus, we are shutting you down.

I KNOW. ETERNITY IS BEYOND MY MEANS. BUT I HAVE A CHILD....

It is metal... no, flesh!

KILL IT

CLUNK... CLUNK..

I AM ALIVE!

Gasp...

A family again, at last...

I AM ALIVE

Train d'Amour

Les

Gaol

Hill d'Amour

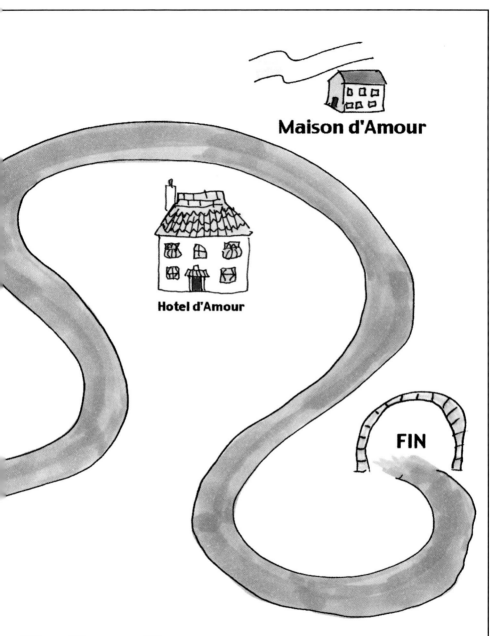

Maison d'Amour

Hotel d'Amour

FIN

Valseuses

Next Morning

- sigh -

Snore

zzz

Then

BANG

She shot herself in her tunnel d'amour

Hotel

DANA DANA

How Romantic

Welcome back

Then she died boo hoo hoo

She had a son in jail. Let's meet him on his release

I'll sleep with him

SLAM

Next Day

What a Man!

Big Deal!

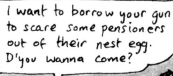

I want to borrow your gun to scare some pensioners out of their nest egg. D'you wanna come?

Sounds safe enough

Isn't he wonderful?

On the Job...

Die, prison warden scum

BLAM

He lied to us!

On the run

And then he shot him dead and we both ran away...

Can we swap cars?

?

!

Can I sleep with your teenage daughter?

ciao

au revoir man

tea time, dear

Wonder what's next?

Apocalypse

Saigon

Playboy Country

Bridge　　　　　　　　**Kurtz**

Now

The Beginning

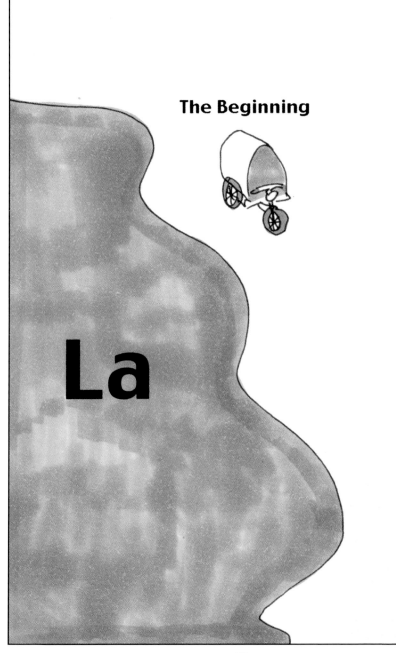

La

Circus

Death of Illusion

FIN

Strada

The Mansion

Women

Nature

Gudrun and Ursula's house

Industry

In

Love

The Absence

The

Last

Birth of Badass

Base

The Brig

Detail

The

The Hospital

The School

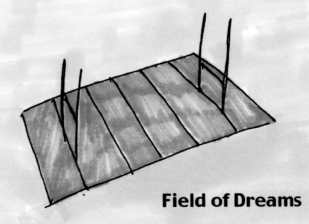

Field of Dreams

Virgin

My House

Their House

Suicides

Le

Le Club

Minimalism

Le Gendarmerie

La Cage

Samourai

The

Monument Valley

Scar's Lodge

The Jorgesens

The Edwards Place

Winter

Searchers

Let's Go Home

Mama's House

The Tullio

Rome

L'Innocente

Africa

9 months later

It is a boy!

Phew!

Whatever!

What's for tea?

That Christmas

You all go off to mass. I'll stay here and look after the baby...

Bye Son

gulp

SNORE

BRRR.. ERK!

God rest ye merry gentlemen

We're home...

MAMA MIA

My Baby!

What a Surprise!

In Private

You killed him!

You wanted him dead too!

In Rome...

..and that is the story. My wife hates me

Babies are robust. It would have died anyway

It is the thought that damns me

Witness the end of the story...

POP!

The Scandal!

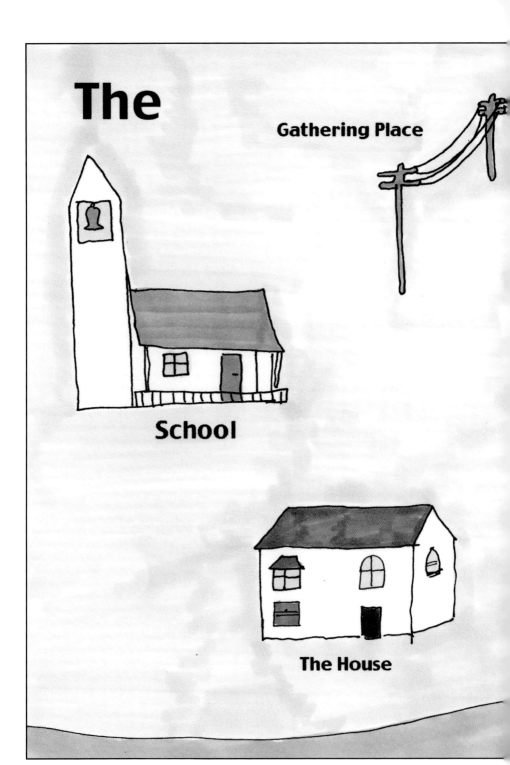

The

Gathering Place

School

The House

First Attack

Birds

Bodega Bay

89

Landscape

Island in A Dream

Robe

Huron Village

Start Here

C'est Chic

The Birthday Party

Uncle

Homework

Nikita

The Way Out

The Caged

Hard

Liberation

Hong Kong Babies

The Sins

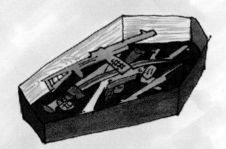

Coffin Mixture

Boiled

Sunset

Wow

Free

Gee Whizz

New

Empire

Fabulous

Great

Donnie

Public Art

Darko House

Pervert House

Love

Illustration

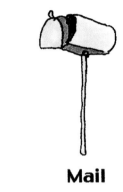

Mail

Prospect

25 Days Remain

I told you to do this!

SCHOOL

I've flooded the school and burnt the self help guys Pad!

The self-help guy at school was the organiser of a kiddy porn ring! The fireman found a 'dungeon'!

Hey - I've become an instrument of God!

Wow, a portal from my chest has taken me to my father's gun!

It's halloween already and the world will come to an end tomorrow. I need to talk to Grandma Death to see how to stop it!

See my mask ha ha ha ha

woo woo-ooh

There she is!

Beep Beep

gasp!

crunch

oops

The Driver...

sorry

erk!

BANG

You killed my Girlfriend!

This is coming together! I'm going to create a time loop and therefore save the world! I am a superhero!

Good Portal Use!

He's going backwards in time!

CRASH

I may die, but the world will now live. I died in the accident afterall!

We're alive.

who are you?

THE END

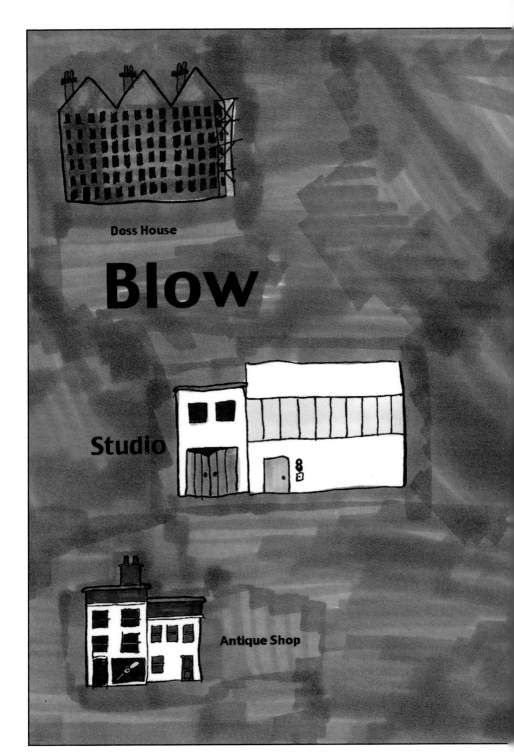

Doss House

Blow

Studio

Antique Shop

Night Club

ENTRANCE

The Park

Up

Home

Meeting Place

Information Point

Hideout

Fargo

The Twin Cities

Beginning and End

Blue

Light

Underworld

Baby sees Mummy

Darkness

Velvet

The Texas

Graveyard

Bone Sculpture

Holiday House

Woodshed

Chainsaw

Slaughter House

Massacre

Raw Materials

The

The Word

Freedom

The People

Fountainhead

Modernism

Panel 1: SLURP
I'll do anything to escape from you. This building is too beautiful. People will ignore your work.

Panel 2: Sure enough...
No one wants to hire me
I'll hire you to build a store

Panel 3: SOON
Everyone wants an O'Rourke!

Panel 4: It's her again
I'm Wynand. Make a house for my miserable new wife.
I'm sooo bored

Panel 5: You're great. Build the highest building in New York.
You got it.

Panel 6: Next day
Whoa. This building project I designed for you has been saturated in a classicism unsuited to its function!
I was always crap

Panel 7: That night
BOOM!
Yes, it was me!

Panel 8: At the trial
My individuality is the greatest value. Modernism is as important as fire, or the wheel. It really is.
How true
Profound

Panel 9: I'm Wynand. My news paper The Banner defends Howard Roarke.
What's the circulation?
About 30
Um... reverse that!
UP ROARKE ↑
DOWN ROARKE ↓
BANNER we were wrong!
ROARKES WON!

Panel 10: I betrayed my friend. Goodbye.
Howard needs me...

Panel 11: Join me on my erection
You Betcha!

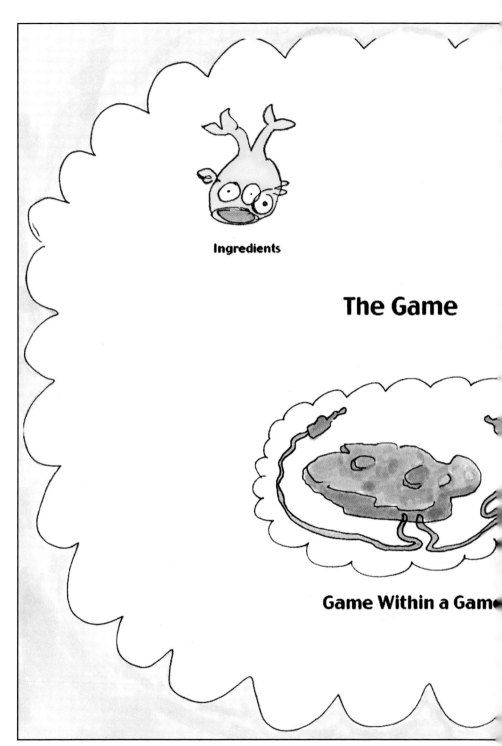

Ingredients

The Game

Game Within a Game

Bullets

Realism

eXistenZ

Let's go to a safe place

Welcome old friend. Make yourself at home

MOTEL

Go to a cabin and play the game ... together!

Your Chinese meal Sir... Arrgh

BANG

You are a spy and you must die

Oh no. The only version of the game is dead

Hang on. We are still in the game!

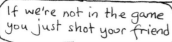

If we're not in the game you just shot your friend

BLAM

Suddenly

Phew, game over everyone! Thanks for playing eXistenZ!

Hey Mr Designer, thanks for letting me play the elusive game Creator in danger

Even if you are the real one...

Then...

BLAM

Death to the Demon Designer!!

Der...are we still in the game?

SECURITY

Hiding Place

Battle

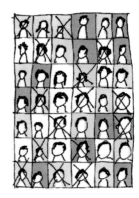
Roll Call

Lucky Dip

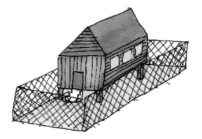
Detention

Happy Families

You are here

Playground

School Dinner

Royale

Wanted

For Murder

Reward

Prize Giving

Hi Class. You know that law where a class is marooned on an island until all but one is dead...

Where are we?

Who drugged us?

Well, you are that class!

You are now on an island...

Now calm down, and watch the video

Welcome to Battle Royale. You will each recieve a weapon and some supplies

YOU ARE HERE

Your neckbands will explode if you don't go where we want – we'll let you know!

Kill each other until there is one pupil left, and hurry up. Good Luck!

I'm scared

What's this on my neck?

Here is how the neckband works any questions?

Whoa

scream!

Get out, one at a time!

Good Luck Shuya

I'll wait outside

Outside

Noriko, over here

Shuya, it's started !

That's for not sharing your sweets

crunch

Run and hide!

23 Left

Morning.. Goodbye Cruel World

Let's hide in this cave until things calm down

crunch

Kids are killing themselves...

136

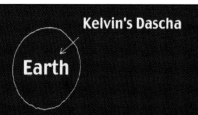

Kelvin's Dascha

Earth

Space

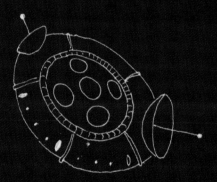

Space Station

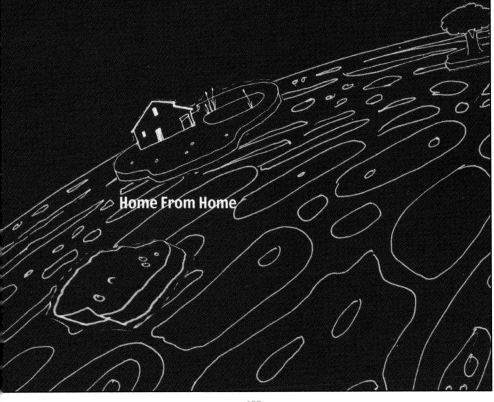

Solaris

Home From Home

On the video recorder...

Hi Kris. I'm dead now. I killed myself. Nuke the ocean. It's a monster.

hmm

Don't kill me Kris. We have made emotional contact

When I close my eyes I can't remember my face

She does not know she is a memory!

In the library

There are three of us left. We all have visitors from our past. It is enough to drive you mad.

But she's my wife

No she's not!

The visitors are part of **the power** of the ocean

Where do I come from? And in knowing me do you know yourselves. We visitors are drawn from your memories

MADNESS WOULD BE A DELIVERANCE

My wife killed herself because I left her

Don't worry. Shame is the feeling that saves mankind

Next Morning

huh?

Hey Kris. All the visitors have gone.

oh

Islands are appearing. It is trying to communicate.

Time to go home?

But I feel great...

Not knowing about death

practically makes us immortal

So...

I love you dad

Er, I'm not your dad.

I would like to thank Julia Bracegirdle for her invaluable
advice and hard work on this project.

I am also grateful to the University of the West of England
research fund and immprint books for their financial
assistance and support.

Special thanks to Keith Sargent for his design input
throughout the preparation of this book.

Wayne Lloyd